BLOTS of INK

Excerpts of Mindful Recovery and Personal Transformation

FRANK GARCIA

Copyright © 2023 by Frank Garcia

All rights reserved. This book or any portion thereof may not be reproduced or used in any manner whatsoever without the express written permission of the publisher except for the use of brief quotations in a book review.

ISBN: 978-0-9600633-5-2

Introduction

Unlocking the Power Within - Embrace Your Journey of Transformation

As an author in the realm of recovery and personal transformation, I have embarked on a mission to guide individuals on the path to becoming the best versions of themselves after navigating the depths of substance abuse. Through my latest creation, "Blots of Ink," I invite you to delve into the internal dialogue that has shaped my own healing journey and discover small, impactful word tracks that can ignite profound change within you.

Within the pages of this booklet, you will find a collection of intimate reflections and thought-provoking insights carefully curated to shake the foundations of your mindset. Drawing upon my individual experiences and the triumphs of those who have walked similar paths, "Blots of Ink" serves as a compass, gently guiding you towards a future of resilience, growth, and purpose.

Each blot of ink within these pages holds the power to rewire your thoughts, empowering you to overcome obstacles, heal wounds, and rewrite your life's narrative. This collection serves as a steadfast companion, providing a source of inspiration, love, and empathy as you embark on your own transformative journey.

As a fellow traveler, I understand the challenges and triumphs that await you on this path. "Blots of Ink" serves as a testament to the resilience and unwavering belief in the power of personal transformation. It is an embodiment of the wisdom acquired through traversing the shadows and emerging stronger, wiser, and more self-aware.

Within this sacred space of reflection and healing, you will discover the solace of knowing that you are not alone. "Blots of Ink" unites the voices of countless individuals who have faced their demons, embraced their vulnerability, and emerged with a renewed sense of purpose. Their stories, combined with the transformative power of carefully crafted word tracks, will serve as beacons of hope and catalysts for change.

Welcome to "Blots of Ink." Let the journey begin.

Recovery

Please remember
that recovery
allows us to
take back our
lives. It's not a
clique, fad, or disguise,
but a guided
return to one's
own normalcy of
mind, body, and soul.

Is healing for you?

I get that we
all heal different
yet, please remember
that when you
own a bad decision
VS a "mistake"
your accountability log
gets upgraded,
and thus true
healing begins and
you'll no longer
be nursing a scab.

A Gentle Reminder

Only to the degree
that you love
and care for yourself,
is equal to the
degree that you
can love and care
for others.
You are first always,
it's for your own safety.

The benefit of you first

When you put
yourself first,
you can then
offer others the
best of you, If
you don't, well then
you can only offer
them whatever's left.

Healing together

Good day,
the words fear,
shame, and guilt
were introduced to
us in school, but
just because they
were taught to us
by a teacher doesn't
mean we keep
fostering the relationships.

Be Cognizant

Today was made for you. Be careful what you think or dwell upon. Always remember that where your mind goes your body will surely follow. Be very aware.
You matter!

You Know

All throughout today,
simply make the
next best decision!
You will more than
likely always have
two choices, maybe more.
so, choose which is best
for you, you'll know.
Do it for you!

Let it go!

You can continue
to let that "thing"
bug you, eat at
you or even rent space
in your head for free,
but why? Let it go, and
welcome your freedom back.

Friend or Foe

If you have
liabilities instead
of assets within
your contacts,
well then you
know what to do next.
Hint-Delete them

As we heal

In our depressive
states, it's growth just
getting to the front
door of the house.
For today, go open
it and sit on the porch.
In our anxious
state, It's growth
just to sit down
and don't worry.
For today, just
manage only what's
directly in front of you.

Not our Friend

Our brain does
It's best to negotiate
with us all day long.
The question is,
who is winning more,
you or your brain.
Growth is in the
harder things.

No offense

Remember all words
are dead until
we the reader,
or listener give them life.
Power, or powerless,
learn not to take
offense for what
doesn't apply to you.
Keep focused.

On Alert

Beware of the illusionist
and the magician,
for "they" are both
one in the same
and neither was
taught to lead you
in the right direction.

The Process

Your process is
100% your process.
The key in recovery
and personal
transformation is
to at least have
that process.

Doesn't matter.

It doesn't matter
What he or she said.
It doesn't matter
what he or she did.
What does matter
is what are you
going to do about it and
is that the best move for you?

An Angles roll call.

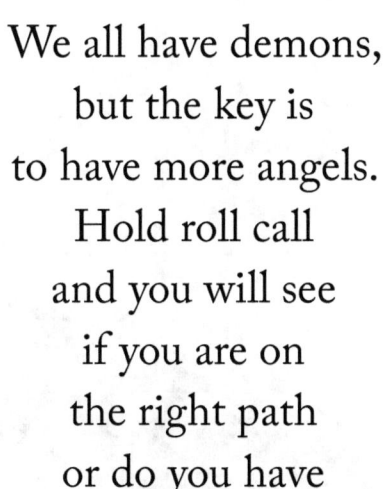

We all have demons,
but the key is
to have more angels.
Hold roll call
and you will see
if you are on
the right path
or do you have
more work to do.

Envision It

Who and what you
are today, are what
you previously envisioned.
If you are unhappy
or seek change,
then simply envision
the next best you
and go after it.

Today

Just for today
focus on what is
good in and around
your life and kick away
the other thoughts.
Today was made
for you before
you were born.
Make something of it.

One Life

"WE" had someone write the beginning of our lives. "WE" most often allowed others to write the middle. Can "WE" agree that "WE" will write the ending? Rewrite your next best you.

You

If you have taken
a moment to read
this then you must
know that you are
of tremendous value.
Remember, your worth
Begins and ends within you.

You Exist

Today does not
exist without you.
This world means
nothing without you.
My words mean
nothing without you.
So, as you can see,
you are the most
important piece
within life's puzzle.
Thank you for you.

Healing

I love you
because I can.
I'll love you
until you can.
Pay no attention
to our degrees of
separation and your heart
shall warm with joy.
Smile.

With Care and Candor

The bad boy within
has never left.
I simply choose to
keep him under lock & key,
thick steel doors,
and a straitjacket.
Do us both a
favor and don't push me.

Fine China

Sometimes we are
so broken and the
pieces are everywhere,
but if we can rise up
once more and look
around, we will soon
discover what's
needed for a comeback.

No Apology

My imperfections are
like bruises on
the finest of fruits,
you can cut them all out,
but soon you will
discover that there's
nothing left to appreciate.
Think about that.

Broken

After years of putting
myself back together,
I've noticed that
the materials used
are of higher quality.
It must have
been the timing,
and thank you Jesus.

Our Fault

When we find that
people are disappointing,
that's on us.
We have either given
them too much credit, or
do we think we are
so much better?
Think about that.

Forgiveness

Thinking about "It"
or "Them" is ok.
Focusing on "It or "Them"
is unhealthy.
Not forgiving "It"
or "Them" is mental
and spiritual death.
Healing does get
easier once you
have chosen to forgive.
Forgive sooner so that
You can live longer.

Soulmate

To love is hard.
To hate is easy.
To fully surrender
yourself to another,
well, that's just
some next level
sh** right there!

Let's care more!

If you notice
another person having
thoughts of shame,
guilt, or fear,
lend a hand.
You never know,
that can be you some day.
Care a little more
and be the difference.

Getting well

Depression wears many
disguises and lurks.
Chameleonize yourself
in love, forgiveness,
and grace from God.
If your heart exudes the above,
that darkness won't
even recognize you anymore.

Why not to judge?

Because you are not them.
Nine out of ten times
you don't know the
whole story and last
you don't have wings,
or a halo on your head.
Worry about yourself.

Live

Life will come and go.
We will come and go.
What memories and
with whom will
you make in-between?
Think about that.

You first

To the degree
that you can love
yourself is equal to
the degree that
you can love others.
It all starts with you.
Keep topping off your cup,
so, it will spill over onto others.

Offer up!

I'll do it! Is the chant of a winner.
I'm in! Is the chant of a winner.
I got it! Is the chant of a winner.
Now, let it be known
that **I hurt**,
I'm scared, and
help me are also
chants of a winner.
Help others heal by caring.

Think about it.

If you are going
to point fingers,
I highly recommend
you do it towards
the mirror or when
giving someone directions.
My advice is, just don't.

Please

Do yourself a favor
and simply research
the meds you or a
loved one is taking,
then decide with
medical advice if
they are working
for or against
your true healing.
Spoiler alert,
you may be shocked.

Pain

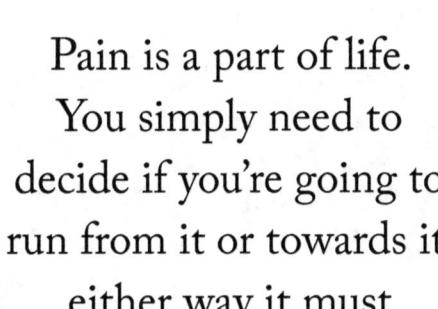

Pain is a part of life.
You simply need to
decide if you're going to
run from it or towards it,
either way it must
be processed.
Hint-If you choose to run
towards it,
it loses its momentum.

Forward and Upward

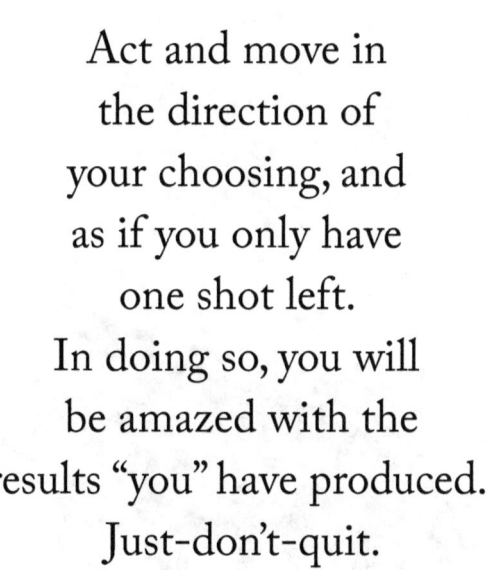

Act and move in
the direction of
your choosing, and
as if you only have
one shot left.
In doing so, you will
be amazed with the
results "you" have produced.
Just-don't-quit.

Universal Compliment

Every time life
appears too hard,
stand up, and know
that this is a compliment.
That entity had to muster
up enough strength
to go up against YOU.
Think about it.

Today

Have your plan.
Ask more of yourself.
Be decisive.
Move towards love.
Process only what's
in front of you.
Think forward and
never look back.

Love

We **need** to love ourselves.
We **can** love others.
We **should** love our enemies.
We **are** what love is,
can, and should be.
Let's help each
other spread love today.

Boundaries

If at any time you
feel that someone is
wasting your time,
they're not,
they are simply doing
everything that you
have and are
allowing them to do.
Cut them off.

Art of 3 P's

Have a **Process**.
Practice **Patience**.
And await the **Progress**.
It is simply how I
have chosen to function.
Try it.

Go

Go big or go bigger,
you can even just
go, but no matter what
you choose, just
don't go backwards.
I believe in you.

May I?

To love is a privilege.
To be loved is an honor.
Yet, in recognition of both,
you must be able
to love yourself to
see their true gifts.
Let's heal together.

Projective thinking

Live, as if there is no tomorrow.
Love, as if you have ten hearts.
Do, as if you can't fail.
The best you awaits
as if it knew no better.
We create our future.

Awareness

Those who try
to take your spot,
your light, or
your happiness will
only be successful if
you allow them.
Those who have
no plan will always
try to make you theirs.

Step by step

If you can stick
to walking your walk,
no matter how fast
your enemies run,
they will never catch you.
Think about it.

It's up to us.

No expectations and
no judgements, allows
me no disappointments.
Make the choice for
a better mindset, and
you've made the choice
for a better quality of life.
Let's heal together.

Because you matter

If you're ok
with being average,
then keep doing it.
If you're ok
with being ok,
then keep doing it.
If you're ok
with doing the minimum,
then please keep doing it.
If you're still reading,
then get comfortable
with being uncomfortable.
Do what's hard and go be great.

Conclusion

Within the realm of "Blots of Ink," you have discovered the power to create change within you. You are not just a mere observer of life's tapestry; you are an artist with a canvas before you, and the strokes of your actions can paint a masterpiece that leaves an indelible mark on the world. You have the strength to mold your destiny, and with each step you take, you inch closer to turning your dreams into reality.

Remember that you are loved, cherished, and valued beyond measure. As readers of "Blots of Ink," you have seen a glimpse into my soul, and that vulnerable connection unites us. Embrace the realization that you are never alone in your journey, for countless others share similar joys, struggles, and aspirations. Let the knowledge of this shared humanity foster empathy, compassion, and a sense of belonging.

In the silence of contemplation, you will find the echoes of your truest self. Embrace the moments of solitude, for it is within this sanctuary that you can discern your purpose and ignite the passion that fuels your heart. Your unique voice, like the ink on these pages, is a gift meant to be shared with the world. Let it resonate loudly and fearlessly, for your story matters.

As you close this chapter and look to the horizon, remember that each new day brings an opportunity for growth and transformation. Life is an ever-unfolding narrative, and you are the protagonist of your story. Embrace the uncertainties and challenges as catalysts for growth, for it is through adversity that resilience is born.

Know that you have the strength to overcome any obstacle, the power to inspire change, and the capacity to bring joy to others. Your actions, however small they may seem, have a ripple effect that reaches far beyond your immediate surroundings. The love you share, the kindness you extend, and the passion you ignite have the potential to change lives, uplift communities, and shape the course of humanity.

So, dear reader, go forth with unwavering courage and a heart full of love. Embrace your authenticity, for it is the source of your strength. Let the pages of "Blots of Ink" serve as a reminder that you are a force to be reckoned with—a beacon of hope and a catalyst for positive change.

In a world that sometimes seems daunting and vast, remember that you hold the power to make it better, to touch hearts, and to leave behind a legacy that transcends time. As you close this book, step into the world with newfound purpose, armed with the knowledge that you are overwhelmingly powerful, loved, and ready to take on the world.

Your journey has just begun, and I can't wait to see the beautiful stories you will write with your life. Keep daring, keep loving, and keep shining your unique light, for the world awaits the extraordinary impact only you can create.

With boundless hope and admiration,

www.ingramcontent.com/pod-product-compliance
Lightning Source LLC
LaVergne TN
LVHW051526070426
835507LV00023B/3329